School Counselor's Scrapbook

By Janet M. Bender, M.Ed.

A Collection of Bulletin Boards, Small Group Activities, Arts, Crafts, and Creative Props for Grades K-6

ISBN-1-889636-44-4

Library of Congress Number
2001099473

10 9 8 7 6 5 4 3
Printed in the United States

youth light
inc.

PO Box 115 • Chapin, SC 29036
800-209-9774 • 803-345-1070 • 803-345-0888 fax
yl@sc.rr.com • www.youthlight.com

Dedication:

In memory of my father,
James P. McAlpine,
a great creative thinker.

Acknowledgements

I would like to thank the following people for their contributions to this book:

To God
for blessing me with ideas
and leading me to share them with others.

To my creative daughter,
Amy Manning,
for her affirmation and encouragement.

To my husband,
Frank,
for his loving support and
patience throughout this project.

About the Author:

Janet M. Bender, M.Ed. is a 30-year veteran teacher and elementary school counselor with a graduate degree from The Citadel in Charleston, South Carolina. She received her bachelor's degree in Elementary Education from Winthrop University in Rock Hill, South Carolina.

She currently does full time writing, consulting, and community workshops in the fields of elementary counseling, parenting and outreach to children. She is the author of *Ready... Set... Go! A Practical Resource for Elementary Counselors.*

She has been recognized for her contributions to the counseling profession through numerous achievements and awards. In 1998-99, she was named Counselor of the Year for Dorchester II School District in Summerville, South Carolina.

About the Scrapbook:

This "user friendly" collection of bulletin boards, small group activities, arts, crafts, creative props and magic tricks, provides easy-to-follow instructions and reproducible patterns for spicing up your counseling program with visual, creative materials and activities. Students will have fun while they learn with these "hands on" activities.

Table of Contents

INtroDuctioN

Believe it or not, I like doing bulletin boards. In every school I have worked in, I have been responsible (my choice) for maintaining a hall bulletin board. For me, it adds variety and creativity to my job as well as serving as an effective visual means for teaching and reinforcing guidance monthly themes and objectives. Positive motivation and public relations is another advantage of having a guidance bulletin board.

Realizing that many counselors do not enjoy this part of the job for a variety of reasons, I have attempted in the first two chapters of this book to provide interesting, yet user-friendly samples of some of the displays I have used.

Chapters 3-6 focus on arts and crafts for small groups, props and tricks to use with small or large groups, motivational awards and behavior contracts, and ideas and displays for school-wide projects.

My intent is to share tested ideas that will add a creative touch to your guidance program, and provide meaningful aides for getting lesson goals across to students. Just as "pictures speak louder than words," hands-on activities help most learners retain information better. Additionally, inviting students to become involved in fun, creative activities leaves them with a positive attitude toward the counseling experience while meeting their goals for personal growth.

Janet Bender

Chapter 1:

Bulletin Boards with Monthly or Seasonal Themes

I use bulletin board displays in several ways: to incorporate guidance objectives into seasonal themes, to reinforce monthly classroom lesson themes, to display student work, or to spread positive messages about school-wide events. This chapter contains a sampling of monthly displays that incorporate seasonal themes.

August/September

This simple **"Welcome Back"** bulletin board might be used to greet students the first week or two of school. Poem is centered on a cut-out resembling a chalkboard or a computer screen with greeting words (hello, hi, good morning, buenos dias, howdy, hey, etc.) cut out of different colors and fonts placed around it. Add a school days type border and you're "good to go." Pictures of school-related items such as globes and books may be added.

"Smooth Sailing Ahead: Let Guidance Light the Way!"

(This sail boat can be used with lots of different captions such as:

- "Sail into September with Good Work Habits" (add fish with habits written on them)

- "Sail into Success with a Good Book!" (see May)

- "Sail into Successful Seas with Good Study Habits"

- "Sail into Success with Character Education" (write character trait on flag each month)

The wording on the flag can be changed to fit the theme you choose. For a 3-D effect, stuff crumpled paper behind the large sail, or curl ribbon or paper strips for waves.

"A Smile is a Curve That Sets Things Straight"

"Start the Year with a Smile"

This bulletin board looks cute with a smiley face border if you have it.

Eye lashes are made from strips of black construction paper curled

around a pencil to give a 3-dimensional effect.

"Set Goals for a Winning Year"

Take advantage of students' interest in fall sports with this display. You can choose goals to write

on footballs such as: study hard, read every day, always do homework, arrive on time, etc.

October

"Good Deed Tree" (autumn)

Cut out and display a tree trunk and branches on the wall or bulletin board. As a follow-up to a lesson using the book *The Giving Tree* by Shel Silverstein, let each student cut out an autumn leaf and write a good deed they have done or plan to do for someone on the leaf. Attach the leaves to the bare tree in the hall for all to see.

"Counselor's Good Apples"

This bulletin board can be used in a variety of ways. It may be used
to recognize students chosen by their teachers for modeling positive behaviors
such as good citizenship, designated character traits, conflict management skills,
improved behavior, etc. Polaroid pictures and names of students are placed on
apples and changed weekly or monthly depending on your program.

The Counselor's Good Apples

November

"Study Habits to Gobble About"

This bulletin board reinforces a classroom lesson on study skills. Make turkeys on poster board using brown, orange, red and yellow markers, or cut parts of turkeys out of colored construction paper. Pennants look nice cut from red construction paper with black pipe cleaners or rolled up strips of black paper for "sticks." I used a red caption on a white background.

December

"Gifts from the Heart"

Cover different sized pieces of cardstock with Christmas wrapping paper.

Cut out letters or write words on large gift tags.

"Give Hugs and Other Warm Fuzzies for Christmas"

Make fuzzies blue, purple and red with black wings. Letters of "HUGS" can be striped, dotted and checked. Post Warm Fuzzy poem under purple words (warm fuzzies) and on purple construction paper mat.

GIVE

HUGS

AND OTHER

WARM FUZZIES

FOR CHRISTMAS

Warm Fuzzy time is here again,
So shake a hand or share a grin.
Write a note or give a hug.
Tell a friend how much you care.
Use kind words, and try to share.
The more you give, the more you'll get.
Warm Fuzzies are the best gift yet.
So even when this season's gone,
Your "fuzzy" feelings will go on.
—J. Bender

*Warm fuzzy creature adapted from TA for Kids, Alvyn M. Freed

January

SLIDE

Into the New Year With Good Study Skills

"Slide into the New Year with Good Study Skills"

Aluminum foil makes a realistic slide. This slide can also be used

with the caption, "Don't Let Your Grades Slide."

"These Make You Unique"

Using pattern and instructions on the following page, let students make individual snowflakes. Emphasize that each of us is as unique as each snowflake. Put up this bulletin board in the hall to support your lesson.

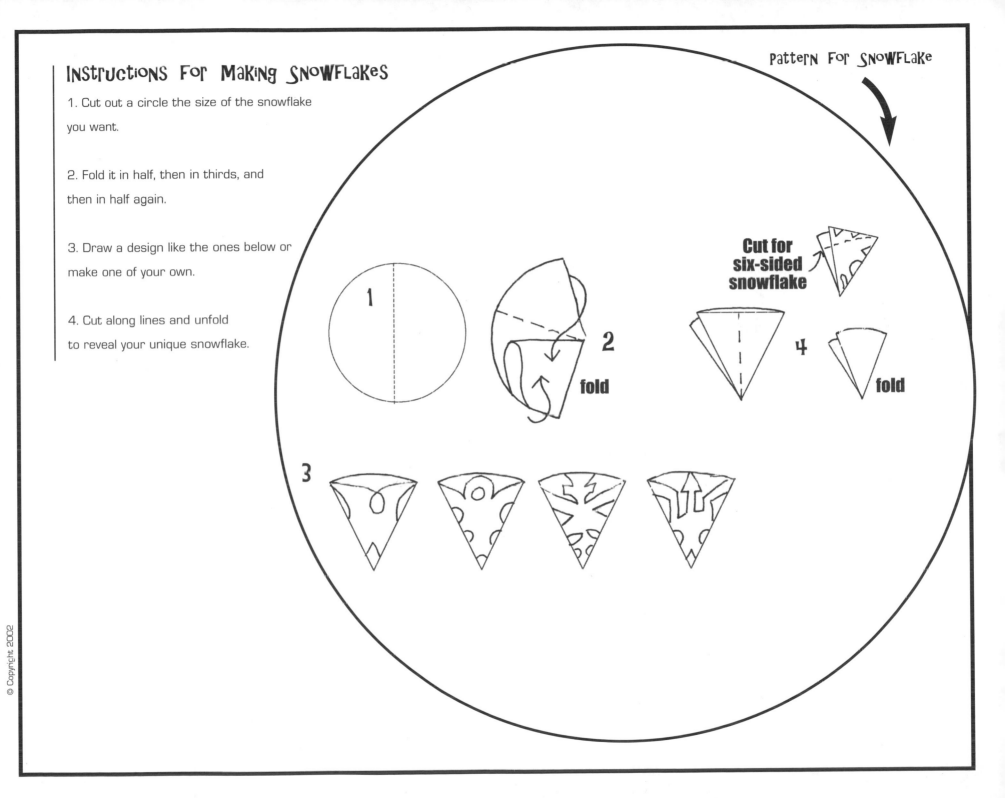

Instructions for Making Snowflakes

1. Cut out a circle the size of the snowflake you want.

2. Fold it in half, then in thirds, and then in half again.

3. Draw a design like the ones below or make one of your own.

4. Cut along lines and unfold to reveal your unique snowflake.

pattern for snowflake

1

2 fold

Cut for six-sided snowflake

4 fold

3

© Copyright 2002

"New Year, New Attitude"

Cut out huge numbers for the new year. Cut out colorful confetti shapes and write positive actions on or near each such as: lend a hand, welcome newcomers, listen, play fair, do your best, share, speak kindly, control your temper. Add twists of crepe paper streamers, a real paper horn, and balloons.

February

"National School Counseling Week"

Make a pie graph with 7 pieces. Cut out matching colored pie pieces. Attach photos on each piece showing the following: individual counseling, small group, classroom guidance, coordination of a school-wide project, teacher/staff support, professional development, and parent education. Use pieces of yarn to connect pie pieces to the whole. Write labels on whole pie to match pieces. Add "crust" and spatula or pie server cut from construction paper.

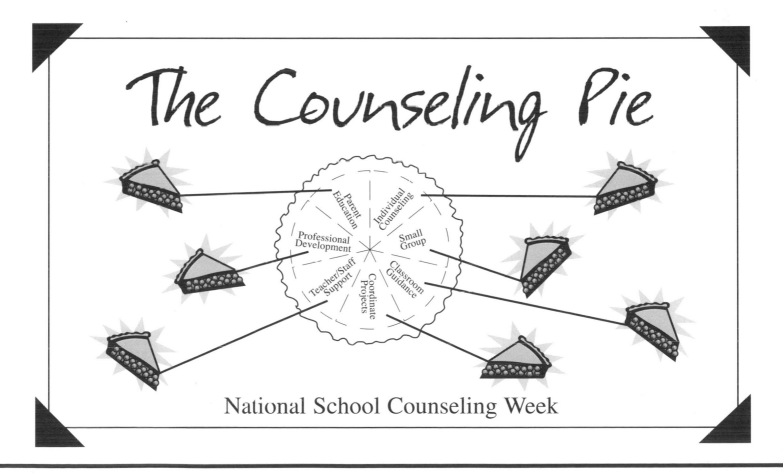

The Counseling Pie

National School Counseling Week

"Hearts United Grow Stronger"

Cut several large hearts out of red construction paper, and several slightly larger hearts out of comics or coordinating wrapping paper. Cut out and decorate white letters of "HUGS" and decorate in stripes, dots, hearts and stars with red, pink and purple markers. You can draw faces on hearts and group them in overlapping pairs or groups of three like balloons. Balloons could have yarn string joined with a bow. School-wide celebration of National School Counseling Week could emphasize ways of showing kindness to others as we do on Valentines Day.

National School Counseling Week

February 4-8

Hearts **U**nited **G**row **S**tronger

March

Successful Students

WHEN THEY DO THEIR BEST

Listen   Get Organized   Manage your time   Complete your work

"Successful Students Bloom When They Do Their Best"

As spring fever strikes, this is a good time to get students back on track

with a reminder of good study habits. Simply cut out tulips and letters in

colors of your choice.

April

"Guidance Helps Chicks Grow Up"

Since April brings Easter/Spring holidays, this display can integrate
the season with positive PR about your guidance program. Border
of colored eggs made by students and some plastic grass will add
festivity to this board.

Guidance Helps
Chicks Grow Up

"Tame the Testing Tiger"

Since April is traditionally standardized testing month, this board can be used to motivate students and remind them of test taking tips. I also provided card stock book marks for students with these tips as a part of my classroom guidance activity for test preparation. A sample is in Chapter 3.

If You Don't Know An Answer:

✔ Re-read the question.

✔ Skip it and come back.

✔ Eliminate answers if possible—50/50

✔ Give it your best shot!

✔ Check over your work.

Tame the Testing Tiger

May

If You're Home Alone, Remember...

Think Safety

keep Doors & Windows Locked

Know how to call for help

911

...And Don't Tell Anyone You're Home Alone.

"Summer Safety"

I try to conduct my last classroom guidance lesson on water or latchkey safety. A coordinating bulletin board in the hall reinforces the lesson and is seen by parents as well. Parent handouts or an article placed in the school newsletter emphasizing some aspect of safety.

"Sail into Summer with a Good Book"

Encourage constructive use of leisure time in the summer with this board. You can make fake book covers or borrow some real ones from your librarian. The sail boat pattern used for August can be recycled here if desired.

Sail Into Summer With A Good Book!

Chapter 2:

Bulletin Boards with Guidance Themes

- Character Education -
- Substance Awareness -
- Study Skills -
- Career Awareness -
- Peer Relations/Conflict Management -
- Individual Differences -
- Behavior -
- New Students -
- Self-Awareness/Feelings -

Character Education

The sailboat bulletin board in Chapter 1 can be changed each month by adding a new (character trait) flag to the mast. The following is another sample of a board with a character trait theme:

"Be Responsible...Take Care of Your Pet"

Be Responsible... Take Care of Your Pet.

SubStance AWareNeSS

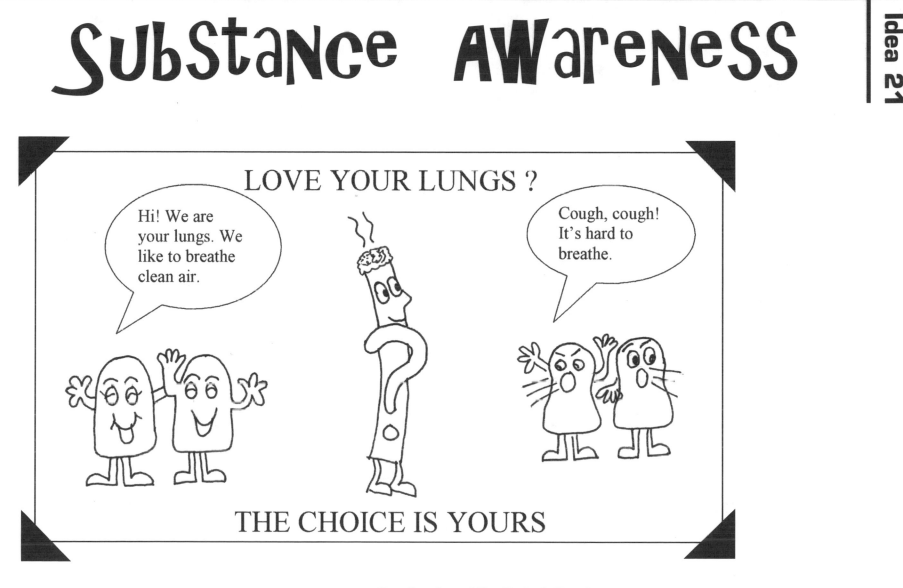

LOVE YOUR LUNGS ?

Hi! We are your lungs. We like to breathe clean air.

Cough, cough! It's hard to breathe.

THE CHOICE IS YOURS

"Love Your Lungs? The Choice is Yours"

Cut out a set of pink healthy lungs and a set of brown unhealthy lungs. Also cut out a tall standing cigarette and a large red question mark.

"Fly High Without Drugs"

This was a winning theme for our "Just Say No" Club float in a local parade several years ago. It emphasizes constructive and fun use of leisure time. Real cloth and yarn may be used in place of paper cut out bows if desired. You could even attach a real kite to the board. A hot air balloon could be used instead of a kite.

"101 Things to Do Instead of Drugs"

Make a 3-D bow and ribbons with crumpled red bulletin board paper.
Collect student pictures relating to this theme and display on red
construction paper matting. This fits in nicely with "Red Ribbon Week."

Study Skills

"Don't Monkey Around... Practice These Good Habits"

The March and the November bulletin boards have study skills themes. This one is good for any month. Make two monkeys. Cut out bananas, write the following study skills tips on them, and hang them on the bulletin board: *Listen Carefully, Do Your Best, Work Quietly, Keep Your Desk Clean and Organized, Ask Questions, Check Over Your Work, Follow Directions, and Bring Your Tools to School.*

Career AWareNeSS

"Free to Become... The Best You Can Be."

Use one large caterpillar and one large colorful butterfly. Then make several smaller butterflies on which to display career picture cut outs. Add black chenille pipe cleaner antennae for a 3-D effect. An added sub-caption could be: **"Explore... Learn... Grow."**

Free To Become...
The Best You Can Be

"Bite into Careers"

Use an apple in three different stages of being eaten, to illustrate the phases of career development from elementary through secondary school. The National Career Competencies for your level could be posted on small apples or on worms around the perimeter of the board.

Bite into Careers

Self-Awareness   Career Exploration   Educational Planning

"Get Hooked on a Career"

School-to-Work objectives in the elementary years focus on self-awareness and an introduction to different occupations. This is a cute display. You can use drawings of careers, hats, or cut out pictures from magazines to place on the fish. An alternative to the fisherman in the boat is a huge hook and line coming from the top of board. Entire board looks like water.

Peer Relations/ Conflict Management

"Be a 'Good Apple' Friend"

Cut out a large red apple and a large green worm and put them on a white background. Use a die cut or pattern to make several red, yellow and green small apples. Write some qualities of a good friend on the small apples and scatter around the board. Friendly acts could include: keep promises, be kind, respect property, be a good sport, give compliments, share, listen, take turns, etc.

IF YOU WANT
A FRIEND,
BE A FRIEND.

"If You Want a Friend, Be a Friend"

Two seals playing ball with each other show cooperation.

Write on the beach balls the words: *smile, help, share, and listen.*

"Keeping Peace in the Hive"

Following up on our classroom lessons on conflict management, we displayed this board using our mascot, the bee, and a review of the main points in the curriculum, *Coping with Confllict.* *

I used this in December, so I made the bees look like Christmas angels. Curled strips of black construction paper or pipe cleaners make good antennae.

Coping With Conflict, (1996) Senn and Sitsch, Youthlight, Inc.

INdiVidUaL DiFFereNceS

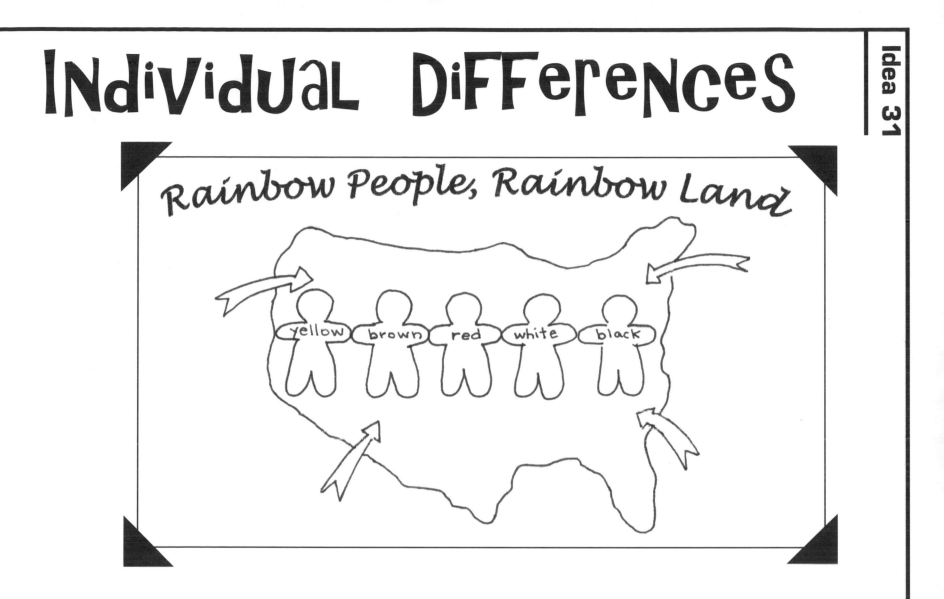

Rainbow People, Rainbow Land

yellow   brown   red   white   black

"Rainbow People, Rainbow Land"

This board highlights the five different races around the world that make up our population. An outline map of the US in green on a blue background is at the center of the board. Cut out five people, one in each of these colors: red, yellow, black, white and brown. Also cut out four large arrows—one each in white, yellow, brown and black to represent the immigrants to America. This board was adapted from an idea in a great booklet of multicultural activities, *Rainbow Activities: 50 Multi-Cultural/Human Relations Experiences*. (Seattle Public School District No. 1, Creative Teaching Press, Inc. South El Monte, CA 1977)

Everyone Smiles in the Same Language

"Everyone Smiles in the Same Language"

Show a variety of children holding hands around a world.

Another option would be to use pictures of children with different handicaps.

"Winning Behaviors"

Use whatever sport suits the season to encourage these positive behaviors. Write the behaviors on basketballs, goals, pennants around the board. I chose darts and adapted the title to read: "Bull's Eye Behaviors."

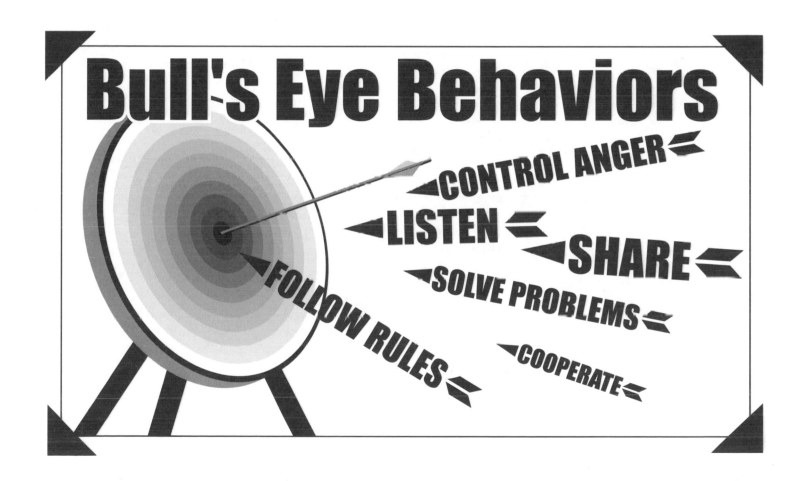

Bull's Eye Behaviors

CONTROL ANGER

LISTEN

SHARE

FOLLOW RULES

SOLVE PROBLEMS

COOPERATE

NeW StudeNtS

"New Kids on the Block"

Draw a picture of your school and different modes of transportation for coming to school such as car, bus, bike, walking, airplane and hot air balloon to make it interesting. When you meet with new students, have them draw and cut out a picture of themselves to add to the board. Let them place their picture on the plane or bus, etc. Change each week as new students arrive. Give old pictures to students to take home.

"Welcome to the Hive"

Our school mascot is the bee, so we consider our school the beehive. One way we welcome and introduce new students is to place their pictures on this bulletin board in the main hallway. Each Friday as I meet with new students in welcome groups, current new students' pictures are added and previous pictures taken down and returned to students to take home. Cut out letters and bees. Draw and cut out a large hive to place in the center of board. Have the students draw self-portraits or take Polaroid pictures of them to place on the board.

SeLF-AWareNeSS/FeeLiNgS

"Feeling Down"

This board reminds students of strategies for expressing and coping with
their feelings. If you want to involve students, have them draw pictures of
faces showing different feelings or have them cut pictures from magazines
to add to the display.

"Chase Away the Blues"

Use a rain cloud, and several colorful umbrellas to give students ideas for coping with stress. Write these ideas on the umbrellas: Listen to music, take a bath or shower, walk the dog, read, call a friend, play a favorite game, exercise, etc.

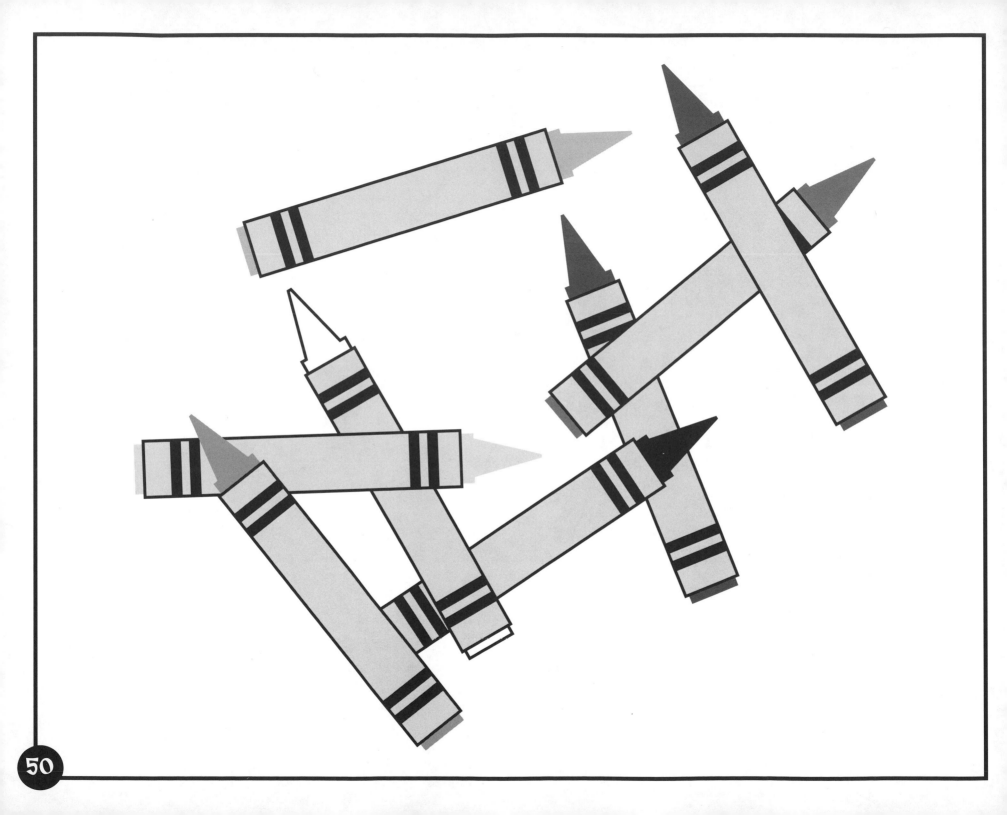

CHapter 3:

Arts & Crafts Activities for Small Groups

In this chapter, I will describe several arts and/or craft activities and make suggestions for using them to facilitate learning within the group counseling process. Hands-on activities serve the dual purposes of involving students in the learning as well as providing visual reminders of the group experience long after the group has ended.

Bead Bracelets/Necklaces

Plastic craft beads come in a variety of colors and shapes. Some are plain and some have alphabet letters printed on them. They can be found in the craft department of most discount stores. Yarn, stretch elastic thread, leather or plastic string, or embroidery floss can be used with the beads. Having a variety of materials allows students of different ages and genders to choose what appeals to them. These are a few of the ways I have used bead bracelets and necklaces.

1) Red, white and blue beads strung on leather can serve as comforting visual remembrances of military parents away from home. During the Persian Gulf conflict in 1991, I held support groups for students whose parents were serving there. I allotted each student a designated number of beads. He/she arranged them in a pattern of their choice on the leather string. I helped them tie a knot in the leather around their arm, or in the case of a necklace, long enough to put over their head.

2) Alphabet beads can be used to spell out student names or initials in self-esteem groups.

3) Beads with hearts on them can be used with alphabet beads to spell out "I ♥ Mom or Dad" jewelry to remember absent parents or loved ones in separation, divorce, or grief groups. If your budget can't afford real craft beads, you can substitute different colored pasta noodles or students can make paper beads from colored construction paper. Cut strips 1/2" X 2" and have students roll them up around a pencil and glue the ends in place. When the glue dries, slide the strip off the pencil. Another type of bead can be made from triangular pieces of paper cut from colorful magazine pages rolled up like crescent rolls and glued at the end. Paper beads may be laced on any of the strings mentioned above. Roll up from left to right. Glue tip to the bead itself.

4) For multicultural awareness or peer relations lessons, have students make one bead each from red, yellow, brown, black and white construction paper to represent the five races which make up the world. String them on several strands of embroidery floss cut long enough to pull on over student's head when knotted. This activity is also a fine culmination to a classroom guidance lesson on individual differences. An excellent source for multicultural awareness activities is *Rainbow Activities: 50 Multi-Cultural/Human Relations Experiences.* (Seattle Public School District No.1, 1977, copyright claimed until 1987, Creative Teaching Press, Inc. South El Monte, CA)

Paper Beads

1 inch

roll up from left to right.

CHeeSeburger BookLetS

I copied this burger pattern (see page 54) from a classroom teacher who had used it in a reading activity. I adapted it for use in a divorce group. We "built" the burger in six weeks by starting with a bun and adding toppings each week. Beside each topping is listed the discussion topic/focus for the week. Below are the six weeks' toppings followed by a pattern to enlarge on construction paper and use with students.

Week 1: Give each student a "bun" bottom and top (manila drawing paper). On the top of the bun, they are to write their name and draw a face for their burger. On the bottom of the bun, they are to write a list of their strengths. Discuss how their strengths help them cope with changes and difficult situations.

Week 2: Tomato or ketchup topping (red). "Hard Things About Divorce." Examples of student responses: "Moving away from my friends." "It is hard to get along with a stepfather."

Week 3: Cheese topping (yellow). "Good things at Dad's." (or "About Dad" if child doesn't visit) Examples of student responses: "We watch movies." "Hunting." "Swimming." "He's nice."

Week 4: Meat (brown). "Good Things at Mom's" (or "About Mom" if child doesn't visit) Examples of student responses: "She helps me with homework." "She's nice." "We go places together."

Week 5: Lettuce (green). "Reasons Parents Get Divorced." Some responses may be: "Stop loving each other." "The bills." "Mom and Dad don't respect each other."

Week 6: Assemble cheeseburger and staple at top. Discuss "Something I Have Learned in Group." Have a party with refreshments to celebrate closure of the group.

Cheeseburger pattern is on the following page. Cut bottom bun on the solid line the size of entire burger. Cut lettuce on dotted line up to top of burger. Cut meat on the x line to the top of the burger; etc. Top bun is the smallest piece. All pieces should layer so that you can staple them together at the top.

My StrengtHS
1. I can sing.
2. I help other people.
3. I'm smart.
4. I roller blade for fun.

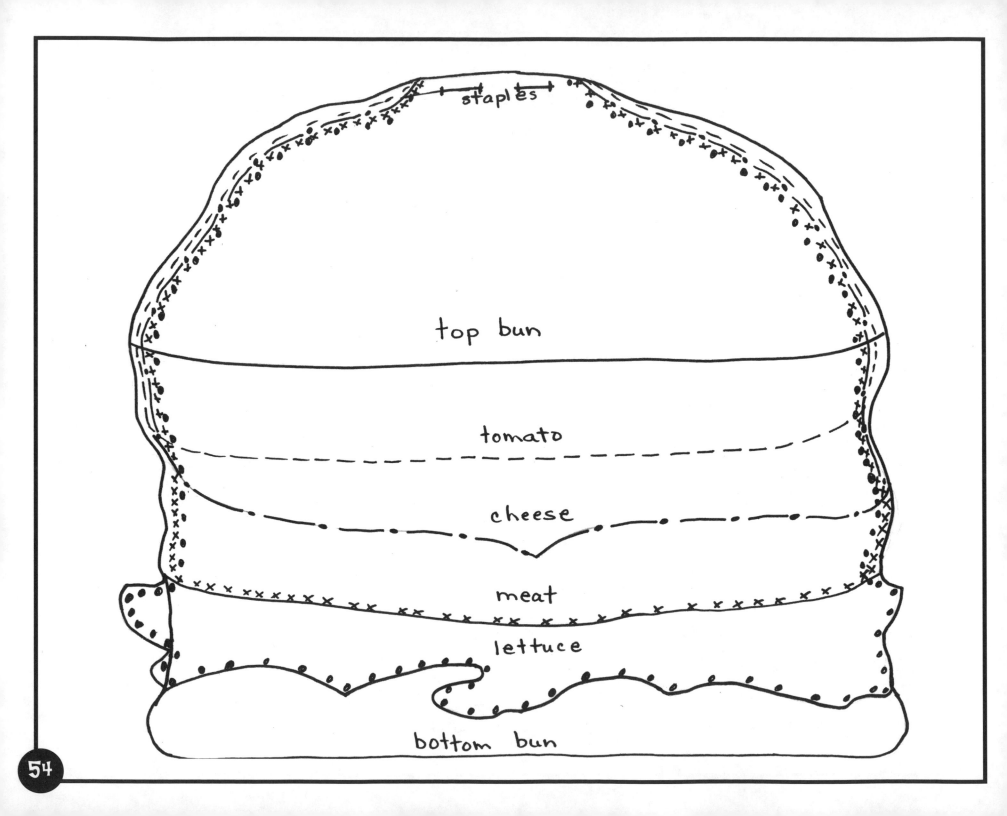

staples

top bun

tomato

cheese

meat

lettuce

bottom bun

PERSONAL PIZZAS

Colorful, construction paper pizzas are fun to make while learning about self-awareness and getting to know others in a group. Give each student a paper plate or a large circle cut from manila or brown construction paper. Cut out and have available a variety of "toppings" cut in different shapes and colors. Cheese, pepperoni, green pepper, sausage, tomato sauce, etc.

On edge of the crust (1/2 inch around) have students write their name and some things they can do well (strengths).

Let students choose their favorite toppings for their pizza. For each topping they choose, they must write on it a positive personality trait that they have. Then they may glue the toppings onto their pizza. If a student has trouble naming traits, let group members help describe them. Sample traits might be: friendly, kind to animals, smart, helpful, etc.

When students are finished, let them take turns sharing their pizzas with the group.

Personal Pizza

I Have Lots of Friends

I Can Read Well

Jon

Braided Yarn "Snakes"

Easy and inexpensive to make, these yarn "snakes" can be used with preschoolers to maintain their attention and give them practice in listening, following directions, and developing motor skills. I use a song from Hap Palmer's cassette tape, "Sally the Swinging Snake." *

I give each student a "snake" that I have made earlier. As we sing along with the music, I model the motions with my "snake" and students follow with theirs. This can be used with a whole class of kindergarten students in a circle on the floor, or with a small group.

Instructions for making snakes:

Cut three two-foot lengths of yarn from your choice of colors. I chose a variegated green so it resembled a grass snake. Place the three pieces of yarn on top of each other and tie a knot in one end. Use a safety pin to attach knotted end to stable object, or have someone hold it while you braid the three strands together. (Right over middle, left over middle, etc.) Tie a knot at the other end. Be sure to remove the safety pin before using.

People Colors

Multicultural awareness can be fostered with the use of "People Colors" paint. It can be purchased from the Lakeshore catalog.* They have 12 different skin colors with catchy names such as *almond, gingerbread,* and *peach.* I prepared a cardboard palate with the 12 colors and their names. Students compare their hand to the colors on the palate and choose the one that most closely matches their skin tone. I give each student a sheet of drawing paper on which to trace one hand. Then I give them a dollop of the chosen paint color on a small paper plate or a bathroom cup and a small paint brush. Students paint their handprint and complete a sentence typed on the page: My people color is _____. This art activity can be used in a lesson on individual differences or self-esteem. In a small group, students can paint their faces rather than their hand if desired.

* Lakeshore Learning Materials, P.O. Box 6261, Carson, CA. (800-421-5354)

Scribble Pictures

Scribble pictures are a great introductory activity to a small group. Explain to students that normally a teacher would ask them to do their best work. However, in this group, sometimes they will be allowed to do their work in whatever way they feel that day. Give students the direction to make the ugliest picture they can make in one minute. Set a timer, provide pencils and crayons, and give the signal to begin. Stop them when the timer alarms. Have students tell why they think their picture is the ugliest. Then have the members of the group vote on the ugliest. Compliment students on their efforts. This activity always brings laughter and helps students loosen up and feel comfortable with a new group. It is especially helpful with students who are anxious or perfectionists. There is a group activity book called *Drawing Out Feelings** which utilizes "scribble pictures" at the beginning and end of each group session.

The Facilitator's Guide to Drawing Out Feelings, Marge Eaton Heegaard, Woodland Press, MN, Feb.1995.

TWo On A Crayon

This activity is fun and helpful in peer relations groups. It reveals leadership/control tendencies in students and fosters cooperation. Pair students up in twos. Give both students in each pair a crayon but only one sheet of drawing paper to share. Instruct one student to be the leader and one to be the follower. Tell the leader to draw whatever he/she wants without lifting the crayon from paper. The follower is to use his/her crayon to "follow in the footsteps" of the leader. Call time after a minute and reverse the roles on the back side of paper. Discuss the importance of knowing when to lead and when to follow and their feelings about each role.

An alternate activity would be to have two students share holding one crayon and making a drawing together.

NaMe Critters

fold

cut

Janet

Name Critters are a good introductory activity in any group, but especially helpful when working on self-esteem building. Model the activity first with your name. Fold a piece of drawing paper length-wise. With a pencil, crayon, or marker, write your name using the fold as the bottom line. Then take a crayon and draw an outline around the shapes of the letters. Cut on the outline. Do not cut the folded side. Open the fold and turn over to see the unique shape made by your name. Ask students to make the shape into a critter using crayons, pencils or markers. Discuss the unique-ness of each name and each person. Display critters with students' permission.

ANgry T-Shirt

Art activities are great expressions of all feelings. In my Anger Management groups, I use this activity along with other expressive ones. After reading a story with an anger theme, I give each student a worksheet with a blank T-shirt drawn on it. They may use crayons, pencils or markers to design a shirt that looks angry to them. Some will draw faces; others may just use lines and colors. Some may even draw an angry looking animal. After drawings are completed, have students take turns sharing times when they have "worn" their angry T-shirt. The T-shirt pattern is to the right. It can also be used to design drug awareness logos or other themes.

MadNeSS MonSterS

Another art activity for expression of anger uses clay or play doh® to form "madness monsters." Give each student a portion of clay. Invite students to squeeze and poke the substance freely. Then instruct them to form a "madness monster." After they have shown their monsters to other group members, let them share what made their monster angry. Finally, encourage students to destroy/crush their clay and stuff it back into its container. I have also used this activity with an entire class as a part of a lesson on appropriate ways to express anger.

Letter Writing

Letter writing is not really an art activity, but language arts expression. It is especially helpful when students have unfinished business with an absent parent, friend, or relative due to divorce, incarceration, moving, or death. In the context of a group discussion, ask students to share what they would want to say to the absent person if they had the chance. Then let them write a letter to that person. They can go through the exercise of reading the letter aloud if they choose. At the end of the session, students may choose to keep the letter, destroy it, bury it in a sand box or leave it with you to keep in a private place.

Bookmarks

Card stock bookmarks are easy to make and serve a dual purpose. In addition to their obvious use in reading, the message (in words or pictures) on the bookmark is a visual reminder of whatever thoughts or skills you wish to reinforce. Cut rectangular shapes from card stock and punch a hole in the top where you can loop a piece of yarn or ribbon. Students can create their own designs or you can reproduce copies of several of your own designs and let them choose one. I have included patterns of some of my bookmarks if you wish to use them.

Bee-lieve in Yourself...
as i bee-lieve in you!
From Your School Counselor

Reach for the Stars!
Mrs. Bender School Counselor

The Magic is in You!
From Mrs. Bender School Counselor

Door Knob Hangers

Students like making door knob hangers for their bedroom doors. I have used them in lessons on study skills, responsibility, and self-esteem. They can be equally effective in small or large group activities. They instill pride in students and can serve as reminders of certain skills or responsibilities. Make copies on colored cardstock and let students cut out. The following patterns may be copied.

's
Pride

Remember...

Lunch
Supplies
Homework
Coat
Book Bag

_____'s
Study Space

My Clean Room

I'm a Responsible Bee!

Paper Chain

Paper chains have been around for many years. They are colorful and decorative, but also useful. Students can write on the strips of paper before making the chain. These are some ideas for things students may write on the chain segments.

adjectives that describe me

hobbies

skills/things I do well

people who love/like me

rules I have learned

things I know/words, math facts, etc.

Chains may also be used as visual reinforcement for appropriate behavior by adding a link each day/time the student is successful with a given task, and working toward a pre-set goal.

My Room Is My Castle

For a sense of belonging, a child's room is a very important place to him/her.

The following house/castle pattern can be used as a 3 dimensional representation of the child's room. On an 18 inch sheet of drawing paper, fold the sides into the middle as shown. Cut the roof to resemble a castle. Let students color the door and exterior of the castle and draw their own room on the inside. Encourage them to add as many details about their rooms as possible. Have students share their favorite thing about their room.

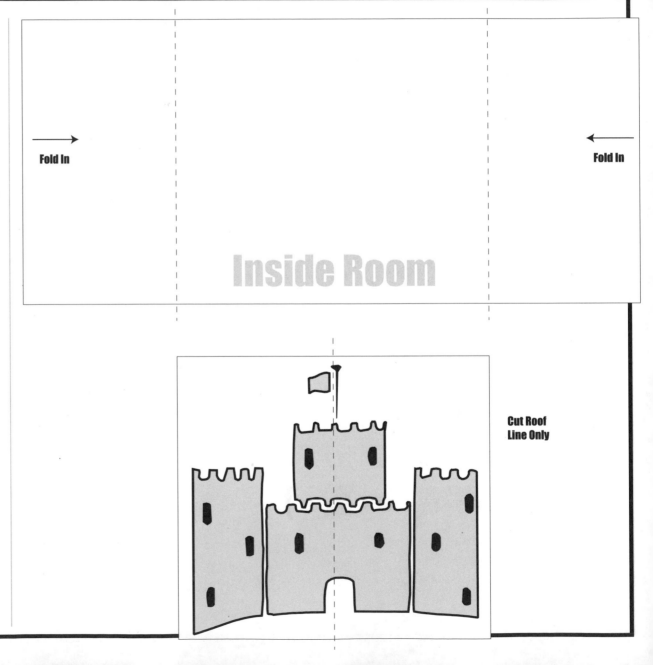

Fold In →

← **Fold In**

Inside Room

Cut Roof Line Only

"I Think I Can" Train

Utilizing the classic story *The Little Engine That Could*, by Watty Piper, discuss the engine's positive attitude and how it helped him get up the mountain. Ask students to share something they couldn't do last year or several years ago, that they can do now. Then ask them to name something that is hard for them or that they haven't learned to do well yet. Enlarge and reproduce the train below. Have them write on the engine things they <u>can</u> do and on the caboose things they will <u>try hard</u> to learn to do.

PeRSoNaL FLagS

After showing students some examples of different types of flags, explain that the pictures and colors on a flag are symbols for the state, country or organization that it represents. Ask them to think about their favorite colors, traits and activities and design a personal flag that represents them. They may incorporate their name or initials if they want to.

Chapter 4:

Props & Tricks

This chapter will introduce you to some simple props, magic tricks, games and activities that can be used with students of any age. I have even used some of them effectively with adult groups as icebreakers, energizers or visual metaphors to emphasize a point.

I will describe a prop or activity followed by a list of possible ways to use it. I encourage you to think creatively and let your ideas expand on these.

DOLLAR BILL
(or $5, $10, $20)

Procedure: Show the bill to students and ask how much it is worth. Then crumple up the bill and throw it on the floor and step on it. Ask students how much it is worth now. Of course, it is still worth the same amount of money. Pick up the bill and unfold it as you share the following:

"You are valuable like this $. Sometimes things may happen to make you feel crumpled and rejected/tossed aside like I did with the crumpled bill. Tell me about a time when you felt this way. (Allow time for discussion.) Remember, just like this $, you are still a valuable person no matter what happens to you. There are some things we can do together to help "smooth out your wrinkles" and help you feel more valuable again."

Suggestions:

- Victim of abuse
- Victim of teasing
- Perfectionist/self-blamer
- Misbehaving, angry, resentful child
- Depressed, hopeless child
- Child of divorce/custody dispute
- Child with low self-esteem for a variety of reasons

WiShiNG WaNd

Procedure: Explain to the students that sometimes things happen the way we would like, and sometimes we wish things were different. Discuss the difference between real and make-believe. Give students the opportunity to hold the wand or lamp and make a wish. Invite students to share his/her wish with you and reason for it. This brief activity can give you valuable information about the child's thoughts and feelings. Follow up with appropriate counseling intervention.

Suggestions:

- Children of separation or divorce
- Child who has experienced loss /grief
- Getting to know a new student

Variations:

1) Make three wishes...one for yourself, one for your family, and one for the world.

2) If you could be any animal for one day, which one would you wish to be and why?

Family Figures

Procedure: Present student/s with a basket containing a variety of miniature family figures (you can include pets if you have them). Ask students to use the figures (I call them "figures" instead of "dolls" so as not to offend the boys) to select their family members and introduce them to you or to the group. Observe selection order, sizes, omissions, placement of people and comments made by students while forming their family out of the figures.

Suggestions:

- Icebreaker, introductions
- Children of separation, divorce, incarcerated parents
- To re-enact incident of abuse, etc.
- To assess self-image (size, color, inclusion, placement of self in family)
- To assess child's perception of who belongs in their family unit

SHOES CLUES

Procedure: Select any type of shoe to show student/s. Use as a catalyst for discussion or written expression. Suggested shoe types are: baby shoes, bedroom slippers, sandals, athletic shoes, dress shoes, hiking boots, ballet shoes etc.

Suggested topics for discussion or writing:

- What paths have these shoes walked?
- How would you feel about wearing this shoe?
- Where would you be likely to go in these shoes?
- Do you have a favorite pair of shoes? Tell which ones and why? (self-awareness)
- What does it mean to put yourself in "someone else's shoes?" (empathy, peer relations)

FLaSHLigHt

Procedure: Using an ordinary household flashlight and a turtle puppet, tell students that you brought your puppet friend to meet them. Have Timmy Turtle keep his head hidden inside his shell. Talk to him about coming out to meet the students. When he still won't come out, ask students what they think is wrong. Possible problems might be that he is shy or scared since he doesn't know them, or because it is his first day at school. He also could be afraid of the dark inside his shell. Ask them if they've ever been afraid in the dark or in a strange place. Suddenly come up with the idea of using your flashlight to lure Timmy out of his shell. Shine the light toward him and have him slowly emerge from his shell.

Suggestions:

- Orientation/ introduction to guidance services as a "light to help students find their way."
- Fear of the dark or unknown
- Spotlight on You! (to introduce students)
- Bright Idea (whatever you want it to be)

PUZZLES

Procedure: Give student an age-appropriate frame puzzle to assemble either alone or with a partner.

Suggestions:

- Rapport building
- Assessing student ability, attention
- Cooperation/Peer relations

CROWN

Procedure: Acquire a cardboard crown from a fast food restaurant or make one yourself from tagboard or construction paper. Recognize a student by letting him/her wear the crown during group or class period.

Suggestions:

- King/Queen for a Day (helper, student of the week, etc.)
- Recognition for participation
- Reward for appropriate behavior
- Self-esteem booster ("You're a winner because..."
- Recognition for skill mastery

Tub Blocks

Procedure: Give each student in a small group the same number of foam block pieces (four or five pieces is good for a small group of 4-5 students). Place a piece of construction paper in the center of the table. Start by placing one block on the "foundation" paper. Ask students to take turns adding a piece to the structure until all pieces are used. Students must do this without talking. They may communicate non-verbally.

Pieces may be placed anywhere within the boundaries of the construction paper. The goal of the activity is to successfully build a structure using all the pieces without making the structure fall. If it falls before all have used their pieces, you can discuss ways to be more successful and start over. Some students will take risks and try to build the structure as tall as possible. Others will be more cautious and spread blocks out on the paper foundation. Leaders, followers, risk-takers, etc. will emerge.

Suggestions:

• Cooperation/Peer Relations
• Icebreaker
• ADD/ADHD, Impulsive Students

Bean Bag Toss

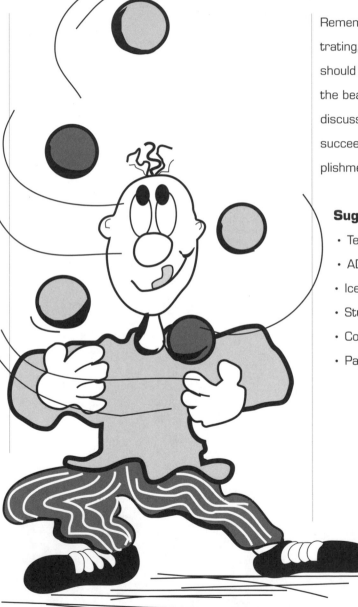

Procedure: One beanbag can be used to designate "turn to talk" in a group. Several beanbags can be used for a group juggling activity. For group juggling, have students stand in a circle with you. Leader begins by calling out one person's name and then tossing a beanbag to that person. That person calls out another name in group and tosses bag to him/her. This continues until last person returns beanbag to leader. Practice this order a couple of times, remembering to call out a name before tossing, and throwing in the same order each time. Ask group if they are ready to try two beanbags. If so, begin the first beanbag. As soon as the receiver has tossed the first bag on to the next person in the circuit, call his/her name and toss the second beanbag. Both bags continue until someone drops one or the leader stops the beanbags. If successful with two, go on to 3 and then 4 at a time. Let group decide each time if they want to try more. If group fails to "juggle" at least 2 successfully, stop and discuss what went wrong and what each person can do to help the group succeed.

Remembering to call names, attending, concentrating, overcoming giggles, team work, etc. should be discussed. If anyone deliberately throws the beanbag too hard or out of reach, stop and discuss gentle tossing and working together to succeed. Students feel a real sense of accomplishment and have a great time with this activity.

Suggestions:

- Team building/bonding
- ADD/ADHD students
- Icebreaker/energizer
- Study Skills
- Cooperation/peer relations
- Parenting workshop (juggling responsibilities)

Feeling Masks

Procedure: Show students a clown doll or clown masks. I have a clown doll with a rotating head—one side is a happy, smiling clown and the other a sad, crying clown. Cardboard masks on craft sticks can be used just as well. I have included a pattern of happy, sad, mad faces. Hold up clown and ask students how he/she is feeling. They will guess the obvious look on the clown's face. Remind students that the clown paints on his/her expression with make-up, so we can't always tell how he/she is feeling by the look on his/her face. Draw the analogy that people, too, sometimes wear one face on the outside but feel another way on the inside. Sometimes we hide our real feelings behind a "mask" so that we won't be embarrassed. Make the point that all feelings are OK. Give examples of times someone might smile to hide sadness, or show an angry face instead of admitting that they feel hurt or sad. (Boys, especially, have been conditioned that it's more acceptable to show anger than tears or sadness.)

Give students an opportunity to hold up two masks—one they show and one that is often hidden behind it. Discuss times when it is OK to have sad or hurt feelings.

Suggestions:

- Students of divorce
- Conflict management
- Peer relations
- Family relations

YOU MAY ENLARGE THESE FACES, COPY ON CARDBOARD, COLOR, CUT OUT AND MOUNT ON CRAFT STICKS.

Games: Don't Break the Ice

Procedure: Regular board games and other games found in toy stores or yard sales, can be used with small groups in a variety of ways. Games can be adapted to suit your topic/needs. One that I use is Don't Break the Ice.® Students take turns using a plastic mallet to hammer blocks of ice out of the whole square. The object is to remove "ice cubes" without making the plastic man (on one square) fall through the ice. I require students to earn a turn with the mallet by answering a question or stating a fact that they have learned during group.

Suggestions:

• Friendship Group (Students must repeat an appropriate greeting to use when meeting a new friend. "Breaking the Ice")

• Study Skills

• Conflict Resolution ("chill out")

• Test Taking Strategies

• Relaxation Techniques

Milton Bradley Game, Springfield, MA. 01101

BubbleS/BallOoNS

Procedure: Soap bubbles with wands, and balloons can be used to help students express anger or frustration. Blowing bubbles requires slowed breathing. Blowing up and popping balloons can also release frustration. Both activities usually turn anger into laughter. Then you can have a calmer conversation with the student.

Suggestions:

- Anger Management
- Anxiety/Stress Reduction
- Group Energizer

My "Worry Bee"

Procedure: After discussion or lesson on stress, have students cut out and assemble their "worry bee" according to directions. Ask students to write their worries on the worry bee. Give them an opportunity to share aloud. Pattern and instructions for making bee follow:

1. Color antennae black.
2. Color the bee body yellow with black stripes.
3. Draw and color eyes, nose, and mouth on the bee's face.
4. Write each thing that worries you on the wings.
5. Cut out the bee parts.
6. Curl the antennae on a pencil.
7. Paste the wings and antennae to the bee's body.

Suggestions:

• Stress awareness/management
• Following directions
• Fine motor skills practice

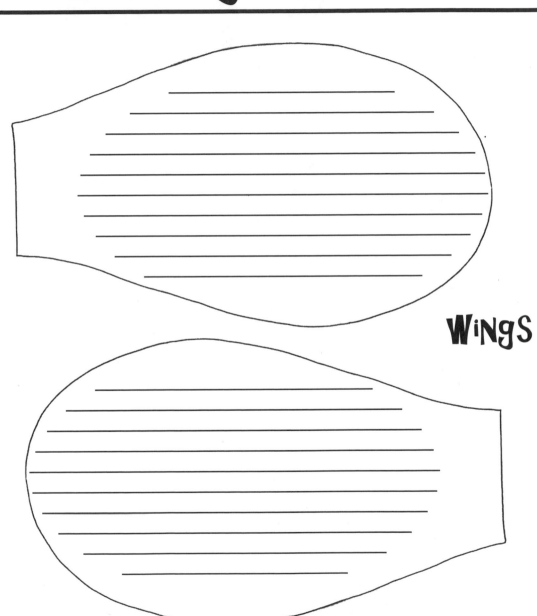

WiNgS

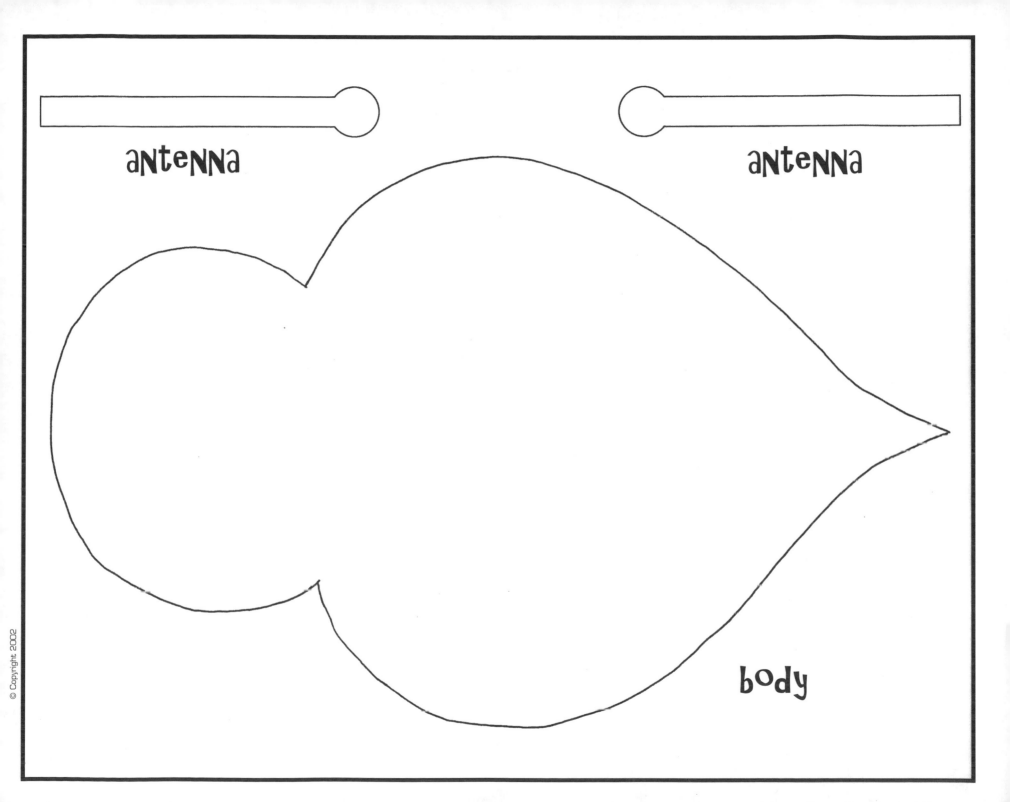

antenna

antenna

body

Caterpillar/Butterfly

Procedure: Use a transforming puppet or make your own from crepe paper and pipe cleaners. To make the caterpillar, stuff a 3-inch ball of crushed paper into green crepe paper and twist to secure at the neck leaving a stem of 3-4 inches of twisted paper. Glue on goggle eyes. Draw on a sad mouth with permanent marker. Cut four rectangular pieces of colorful crepe or tissue paper about 4X6 inches. Gather them in the middle and secure with black pipe cleaner. Do not spread out wings at this time. Wrap this butterfly portion in another piece of green crepe paper and fasten it to the neck of caterpillar with pipe cleaners in three places. These should look like legs. You should now have an ugly, sad caterpillar with a beautiful butterfly hidden inside. Tell your students the following story about Cappy the Caterpillar (story follows). As you get to the end of the story, remove legs and green crepe paper covering to reveal a beautiful butterfly inside. Spread its wings and let it fly to a student as a reminder that we can all grow and change if we really want to.

Suggestions:

- Social Skills
- Self-Esteem

Suggested questions and discussion following puppet skit:

—Would you be Cappy's friends?

—Why was Cappy so unhappy at the beginning of the story?

—What is ugly? What does ugly mean? (unpleasant to look at, bad, quarrelsome)

—What did Cappy learn? What did you learn?

—When Cappy had a problem, what did he do?

- Found someone to talk to
- Thought about it
- Worked hard
- Acted cheerful and friendly
- Believed in himself

—What were some of Cappy's bad habits/behaviors/attitudes that caused him a problem in making and keeping friends?

We all have some "ugly" things about us…things we may feel unhappy about, or things we do that make problems for us. We may talk too much, be too shy, fight or argue or have a bad temper, complain a lot, mope around feeling sorry for ourselves, gossip about others, act lazy with our chores, etc. There are some things we can change and some we cannot. Think about some behavior you have that sometimes gets you in trouble or causes you to feel sad. Write it or draw a picture of it in the ugly caterpillar. Now, think of something you can do to change that behavior into a beautiful butterfly. Write or draw about that in the butterfly. ("I Can Change " worksheet follows.)

Cappy the Caterpillar Grows Up

(Adapted from an oral puppet show by Patsy McCutcheon, Gwen Sitsch and Janet Bender.)

Narrator: Hi boys and girls! This is Cappy the caterpillar, and he's looking very sad today. Let's talk with him and see if we can find out what's wrong. "Cappy, you look very unhappy."

Cappy: I am. Nobody likes me. I was just walking through the forest looking for someone to play with, and all the animals ran away. They said I was too ugly to be their friend. I guess I am pretty ugly. I don't want to be ugly, but there's nothing I can do about it.

Narrator: So Cappy just crawled around by himself until one day he saw Mr. Crow. He thought Mr. Crow was pretty smart, so he decided to talk to him about his problem.

Cappy: Mr. Crow, what can I do? I don't have any friends because I'm so ugly. Nobody wants to play with me.

Mr. Crow: Then, why don't you do something about it, Cappy?

Cappy: What can I do? It's not my fault. If I'm ugly, I'm ugly! That's just the way I am.

Mr. Crow: Oh, no, Cappy. You don't have to be ugly. If you really want to, you can change—but you must do it from the inside out.

Narrator: Cappy thought about what Mr. Crow had said, but he still couldn't figure out how he could do anything about being ugly. He became so unhappy that he began to stay away from others. One day he heard some children playing and squealing nearby. They pointed to him and made yukky faces. Afraid they would step on him, he quickly crawled under a leaf to hide. It was a little quieter under the leaf, but Cappy still couldn't figure out how he could change being ugly. In fact, he couldn't think of anything good about himself. The next day, Cappy heard some birds flying overhead.

Cappy: OH NO! Thoses birds like to eat caterpillars. I must find a safe place to hide.

Narrator: So Cappy climbed up into a tree and again hid under a leaf. Finally, the birds flew away and it was quiet.

Cappy: You know, I really need a quiet place to think. Maybe then I can figure out what Mr. Crow was trying to tell me.

Narrator: So Cappy curled up in a leaf and began to spin silk around himself until he was completely covered in a warm, safe cocoon.

Cappy: Now I am safe, Cappy thought. No one can hurt me in here. Now I'll have time to think.

Narrator: After a while as Cappy thought, he began to feel strange. (Begin taking off pipe cleaner legs.)

Cappy: W-w-what's happening here?! My legs feel weird, like they're shrinking. Whoa, this is heavy stuff! My skin is splitting open!

Narrator: Cappy began to get very restless. He turned and twisted, making the cocoon shake and rattle. Great changes were going on, but Cappy still didn't understand them. Under his cocoon, the furry body, scaled wings, velvet legs, big eyes, and feathery antennae of a butterfly were all developing. With all this growing and changing, Cappy felt scrunched and needed some space. He began to push and pull and pull and push, until finally he broke through the wall of his cocoon.
(At this point in story, expose the butterfly inside the cocoon.)

Cappy: Ahh! What a beautiful day! If only I were as beautiful as this breezy spring day.

Narrator: Just then a gust of wind blew Cappy right off the limb of that tree. Cappy was scared, and as he struggled to catch himself he called:

Cappy: Help! I'm falling and I can't get up!

Narrator: But Cappy didn't fall. He made a remarkable discovery.

Cappy: Hey, I'm flying! I never knew caterpillars could fly. This is great, but what will the others think? Who ever heard of a flying caterpillar? They'll really make fun of me now.

Narrator: But as Cappy looked down, he saw the children looking up at him, pointing and smiling. They were saying things like; Oh, how beautiful! That's the prettiest one I've ever seen.

Cappy: Could they be talking about me? I don't understand. They seem to like me now.

Narrator: Curious to find out what the children found so beautiful, Cappy flew over a nearby pond to catch a glimpse of himself. As he looked at his reflection in the water, he exclaimed:

Cappy: Wow! This is awesome! I <u>am</u> beautiful. Why I am a beautiful butterfly! I'm not an ugly caterpillar anymore. I've got to find Mr. Crow to thank him.

Narrator: So Cappy flew back to the tree where Mr. Crow lived. As he got near the tree, Cappy called out:

Cappy: Mr. Crow! Mr. Crow! Look at me!

Mr. Crow: Well hello Cappy. You sure look happy today.

Cappy: I am happy! You were right when you said I could change. Now I'm beautiful.

Mr. Crow: I knew you could do it. I'm sure it wasn't easy. Not only are you beautiful on the outside, but your new attitude makes you beautiful on the inside too.

Narrator: And away Cappy flew to make some new friends.

I Can Change

before...

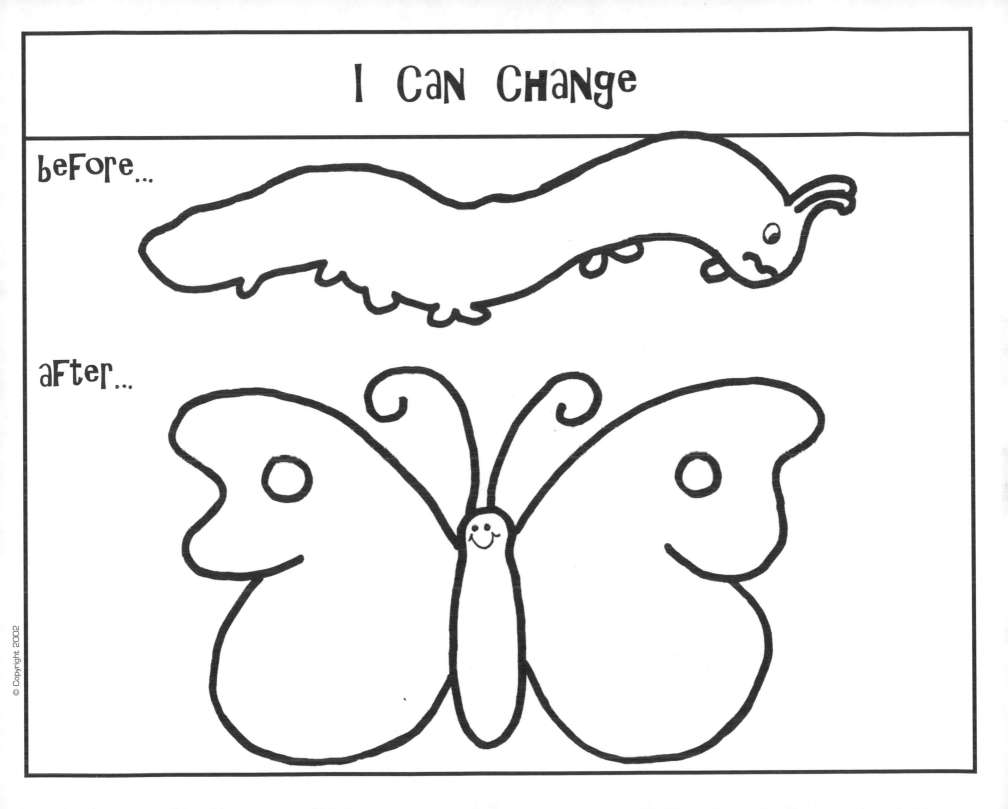

after...

MUSiC

Procedure: Most children love music. I use songs with fingerplays and footplays to teach young children a variety of skills. There are many excellent resources available, but a few I have enjoyed using are:

Fingerplays and Footplays for Fun and Learning, Hallum and Glass, Educational Activities, Inc.1987.

Sally the Swinging Snake, Hap Palmer, Educational Activities, Inc. 1987.

I Have Lots of Feelings and They're Okay, Robert P. Bowman, Individual Counseling Activities, 1997.

Suggestions:
- Pre-school and Kindergarten Classes
- Developmental Play Groups

Sing or Rap a Song about Feelings (Grades K-5)

I Have Lots of Feelings and They're Okay

I have lots of feelings and they're okay.
They jump up inside me every day.
If I was the President, I would say,
I have lots of feelings and they're okay.

I feel happy when I'm with my friends,
And I feel happy when the school day ends.
And I feel happy when I get to play,
'Cause happy is a feeling and it's okay.

I feel sad when I say good-bye,
And I feel sad when a bird can't fly.
And I feel sad when it rains all day,
But sad is a feeling and it's okay.

I feel proud when I bake a cake,
And I feel proud of my new pet snake.
And I feel proud when I stand and say,
"Proud is a feeling and it's okay."

I feel scared when my snake gets out,
Mom doesn't know yet, but she'll find out.
And when she does, maybe then I'll say,
(shout) "Mom, scared is a feeling and it's okay!"

I have lots of feelings and they're okay.
They jump up inside me every day.
If I was the President, I would say,
I have lots of feelings and they're okay.

Magic Tricks

Learn a few easy tricks and adapt them to different lesson themes. Anyone can do the tricks included here. They can be purchased through a local retail store that sells magic tricks. I will briefly describe the trick and possible uses for it.

Breakaway Fan: A beautiful fabric fan opens out perfectly one minute and falls apart the next. It can be compared to broken relationships as in a divorce or to any other situation when things suddenly "fall apart." May be incorporated into lessons on responsibility, family changes, dropping grades, etc.

Magic Light Bulb: This light bulb shines when plugged into your ear. Kids love it. It can be used similarly to the flashlight prop mentioned earlier in this chapter.

Ropes Trick: Three pieces of rope of different lengths are magically transformed to three ropes of equal length. I use this trick in lessons on individual differences or changing behavior.

Wilting Flower: This pretty flower quickly wilts at your command. Great for lessons on feelings. Can also be used to explain how a counselor helps you feel better when you're down.

Magic Coloring Book: [1977, Fun Incorporated, Chicago, IL] This trick is super simple, and very impressive to children and adults alike. As you flip the top corner it shows black and white pictures. When you flip the middle of the book, the pictures are suddenly in color. When you flip the bottom corner of the book, it displays just blank pages. First get really excited and show the children your new coloring book (fan the blank pages). They will react by telling you they don't see any pictures. Then as you are teaching students about manners (magic words), feelings, or conflict managments skills (ways to work it out—share, take turns, count to ten, etc.) you can ask them questions, have them give you information, then toss their answers into the book; watch them become magicians by making the blank pages turn to black and white ones and then to colored ones.

NOTE: A new magic coloring book, "The Magic Coloring Books of Feelings" is now available through YouthLight, Inc (800-209-9774).

Aqua Slush: This powdery substance can turn any liquid into a solid gel in just seconds. A cup of water "disappears" to audience with the help of this magic. I used this in a teacher orientation to guidance. They can observe you pouring water into a styrofoam cup, then poking a knitting needle through the cup without any water leaking out. When you turn the cup upside down without spilling any water, you really have impressed them. My book, *Ready, Set, Go! A Practical Resource for Elementary Counselors,* (Youthlight, Inc. 1999) contains this orientation presentation in its entirety.

Chapter 5:

Motivational Behavior Contracts & Awards

Success Card

There are thousands of resources containing behavior management contracts, awards and certificates. I have included here a sampling of mine. Some can be used individually, and some for an entire group or classroom of students. As a consultant to classroom teachers, it is good to have some ideas to share for improving and encouraging positive behaviors.

Top Flight Pilot

When I was a classroom teacher, I used a bulletin board in the room to display helicopters or airplanes for each student. The board was divided into five levels. Each day that a student achieved the desired behavior, he or she moved their plane up a level. When the student reached the top level on the board, he/she received a certificate, "Top Flight Pilot Award." The next day the student started out at the bottom of the board again and worked to fly up each day. Some students might reach the top in a week. Others might take several weeks to move up 5 levels. The display was an effective visual reminder of the desired goal.

Helicopter Pattern

Enlarge if you wish, and copy one for each student on card stock. Let students personalize with their name and choice of colors.

Top Flight Pilot Award

Presented to

_____

for practicing self-control
as a member of
the room ___ crew.

_____   _____
Flight Instructor (teacher)   Date

Congratulations!

IS a
HIGH-FLYING
STUDENT!

Congratulations!

I'M PROUD OF YOU FOR FOLLOWING CLASS RULES FOR FIVE DAYS!

SIGNED   DATE

Up, Up and OK

Reinforce students who exhibit appropriate behavior or work habits by displaying their personalized kites or hot air balloons on the wall.

Success Cards

Success cards are a positive motivator for group participation and appropriate behavior. Group members agree on a design for their group. Having students choose, cut out and color their cards during the first group meeting also helps them establish a group identity. I usually let the group choose from several sample cards. They must come to consensus on one picture and a name for their group/club. Sometimes this happens quickly and sometimes I have to facilitate a voting process if they cannot agree. I have included here several cards that I have used, but you can enlarge a clip art picture of almost any object the students are interested in and add boxes for stickers. Each week members earn a sticker on their cards for participating and following group rules. Cards are displayed in the guidance office and taken home by students at the end of their group sessions. I have included a few of the more popular cards for you to enlarge and use with students.

Success Card

Success
Card

SSSuccess
Card

© Copyright 2002

GiraFFe Study TipS & ScHeduLe

This is not a contract, but can be used with one. Many students have difficulty organizing their time and environment. This handout can be discussed with student and/or parent and sent home to post and follow.

R-E-A-C-H
for Good Study Habits

Work in a proper environment.

- Quiet place
- Adequate light
- Table or desk
- Supplies

Practice good habits.

- Read with your child/parent regularly
- Drill math facts
- Talk about what is learned at school

Maintain regular communication with teacher.

Seek help with family problems which may affect school performance.

Organize your time. Fill in the schedule attached and try to stick to it.

Let's Get Organized!

Fill in approximate times for chores, dinner, homework, extracurricular activities, bath time, outside play, TV, reading, etc.

GIVE LOTS OF ENCOURAGEMENT FOR EFFORT AND IMPROVEMENT!!

R-E-A-C-H

for Good Study Habits

Schedule

2:30
3:00
3:30
4:00
4:30
5:00
5:30
6:00
6:30
7:00
7:30
8:00 Bedtime

Success Card

1. Listen to and follow directions.
2. Have a smiley attitude.

Reward: _____

	Monday	Tuesday	Wednesday	Thursday	Friday
8:30-10:00					
10 00-11:30					
Lunch					
Recess					
12:30-2:00					
Goal for the Day					

Working cooperatively with teachers and parents to improve student performance is an important part of a counselor's job. Once you have met with the student and adult involved, you are in a position to create a personalized behavior plan to help that student. Students must have some ownership in the plan. One way of achieving that is to sit down at the computer with the student and create a chart to track his/her progress. I let the student choose clip art that reflects his/her interests such as basketball, dinosaurs, etc. I guide them through goal setting and set up a plan that interests them and therefore has a good chance of success. Expectations and consequences are clearly outlined up front. Sample charts follow.

Alex's Success Card

Week of

	Monday	Tuesday	Wednesday	Thursday	Friday
Homework					
Class Work					

Teacher Comments

I will bring in my homework each day.
I will try to complete all my class assignments.
When I check off each, I will earn 10 minutes of extra computer time.
When I get _____ checks, I will go to the treasure chest.

Week of:_____

Larry's Success Card

I will try to

	Mon.	Tues.	Wed.	Thur.	Fri.
Smile!	○	○	○	○	○
Remain quiet during instruction	○	○	○	○	○
Stay in seat unless given permission	○	○	○	○	○
Complete work	○	○	○	○	○
Keep hands to myself	○	○	○	○	○
Share positive statements with others	○	○	○	○	○

Goal for the week:_____

Leap Frog

This is a simple, yet visual way to track behavior. It works well with young or special education students. Decide on a place to display five lily pads in a row. Cut out and laminate a frog with the student's name on it. At the end of each day, the student comes and hops his/her frog to the next lily pad if he/she has achieved the desired behavior in the regular classroom. When the student reaches the last lily pad he earns the reward or privilege. Start over and repeat.

 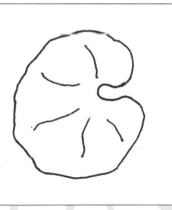 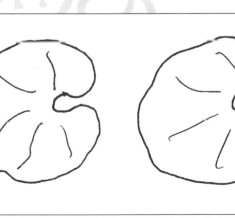

YOu're a WiNNer!

Elementary children love to wear tags, stickers or badges of recognition. You can buy ready-made stickers or make these award tags to tape or pin on a student caught exhibiting a desired behavior.

Congratulations!

You're A Winner!

Badges

Good Work!

Our school PTA owns a "Badge-a-Minit" maker. It was a wise investment with hundreds of uses. During the Persian Gulf War, I conducted support groups for children of military parents. Students made red, white and blue badges or badges reflecting an airplane, submarine or ship that their parent served on. Students wore these badges and their bead bracelets (chapter 3) until parents returned. I have included some of my original patterns. You may reproduce them, make your own, or let students design their own. The possibilities are endless.

I'm not "Purr-fect" But I try hard

(peer Mediators)

Bridge Builders

I'm Shining With Good Attendance!

Friendly Helper

"Tree-Mendous" Work!

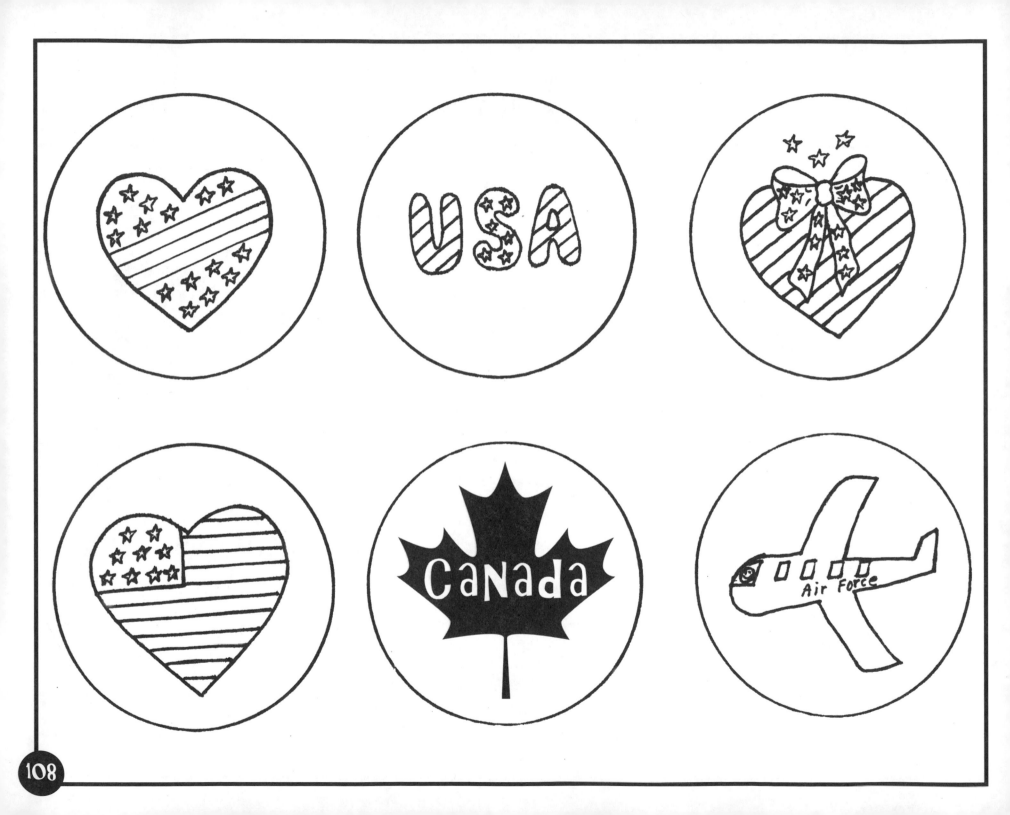

Good NeWS PHONe CaLLS

What? For the month of _____, the counselors will relay good news about students to parents.

Why? ✔ To let parents know that we are proud of and appreciate the good things children do.

✔ To boost self concepts of students thus motivating more positive behavior.

✔ To focus attention on recognizing positive, appropriate behaviors.

✔ To improve community relations.

How? Teacher fills out a "Good News Phone Call" form and returns it to the counselor's mailbox. Make this a special recognition for special behaviors. Don't tell the child that he/she will be receiving it. Let it be a nice surprise. Calls will be made in the early evening when families are more likely to be home. Counselors will note any feedback from parents and return forms to teacher.

Following are some samples of specific "good news" messages. You may want to include good character traits or some of our "conflict management' terms to describe the behavior or attitude.

"John cooperated and showed leadership skills at group time today."

"Susie showed responsibility by remembering her homework every day this week."

"Joe was caring and helpful to a new classmate today."

"Robert prevented a conflict by managing his madness appropriately."

When we call the parents, we will say that we have some good news to share with them from _____(teacher) about _____(child).

"GOOD NEWS" PHONE CALL

Date _____   Child's Name _____   Teacher's Name _____

The good news is _____

_____

_____

Please turn in to your counselor's mailbox at the end of the day. If the family does not have a phone, we will mail a "Good News Letter."

Feedback comments to teacher from parents: _____

_____

_____

_____

_____

_____

"GOOD NEWS"
L E T T E R

Date: _____

Dear _____

_____ and I are pleased to announce that _____
(teacher)

_____

_____

_____

_____

We are proud and know you are!

School Counselor: _____

Teacher Survey
on Good News Phone Calls

We have come to the end of our scheduled weeks for making calls. Please let us know how helpful this program has been for you.

1 Have you utilized the opportunity to have counselors make "Good News Phone Calls?"

     yes   no

If not, why not? _____

_____

2 Have you received any feedback from parents?

     yes   no

If so, explain. _____

_____

_____

3 Have you noticed any changes in student behavior or attitude as a result of calls? _____

_____

_____

4 Would you like for us to continue making calls— either now or in the future? _____

_____

_____

Other comments/suggestions: _____

_____

_____

_____

Please return to your counselor's mailbox. Thanks.

Chapter 6:

Hall Displays & School-Wide Projects

Whenever possible, use hall bulletin boards or wall space to draw attention to ongoing guidance projects and messages. Drug and safety awareness topics, career awareness, and character education are excellent themes for displays. Service projects and student competitions can also be highlighted for students and visitors to the school.

"Grow Through Giving"
Food Drive

On more than one occasion, our school decided to hold a food drive to support local food banks. Since most of their help comes near the fall holidays, we decided to do ours in the spring. We chose a theme, created a hall display to monitor progress, announced a competition between grade levels to see which could bring in the most food items within the designated time (2 weeks before spring break). As food items were counted each day, the stems of flowers in the hall grew taller. We emphasized the fact that people grow in character as they give to help those less fortunate. This is how the project was done. We cut out a large tulip flower for each grade level. At the base of each flower was a box covered to look like a flower pot. The stems were adjusted to "grow" taller each day as the canned goods added up. The visual display was colorful as well as being a lesson in graphing our progress.

(make letters rainbow colors)

Growing Through Giving

1st Grade 2Nd Grade 3rd Grade

Drug AWareNeSS

Bloom Brighter Without Drugs

"Bloom Brighter Without Drugs" was our theme for one Red Ribbon Week. In keeping with the theme, we conducted classroom guidance lessons on substance awareness. The art teacher cooperated by having students create 3-D paper flowers to display in the hallways. PTA volunteers made banners for each class which read, "3-E Blooms Brighter Without Drugs" etc. We ordered 100 red tulip bulbs, divided them among the homerooms (2-3 each), and asked classroom teachers to organize a class outing to plant them in designated prepared beds in front of the school. Teachers had the flexibility to integrate the activity into the lesson of their choice. Location of bulbs was marked with a craft stick labeled with homeroom section so students could monitor the growth of the bulbs. In the spring, we were delighted to discover a mass of red tulips beautifying our school grounds.

Walk Away From Drugs

Each year our school observes Red Ribbon Week (drug aware-ness) with a different theme. "Walk Away From Drugs" was another effective one. Students (either in art class or homeroom) drew, colored and cut out a shoe of their choice. The shoes were dis-played "walking around the walls" of the school.

"Drugs Bug Me"

Another drug awareness theme is "Drugs Bug Me." Students create through drawing, painting, or 3-D art, their favorite bugs to display with the

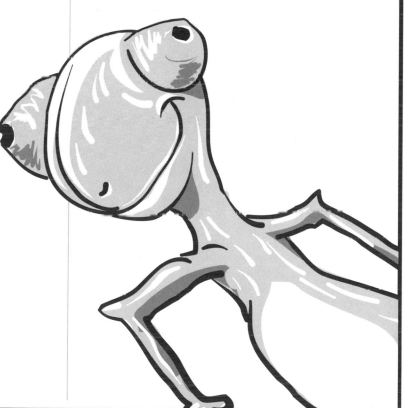

ViOLeNCe PreVeNTiON

"Hands Are for Helping Not Hurting"

This was a PTA generated project to support violence prevention. Volunteers went into classrooms and discussed with students all the helpful things our hands can do. Then they helped students trace and cut out their handprint on construction paper. The handprints were displayed on a bulletin board as a reminder of the positive lesson.

Stop the Violence

We support our local YWCA in their campaign to "Stop the Violence." One simple way to participate is to use a hallway display or bulletin board or several smaller posters around the school. Include the title and information about what behaviors are considered violent. Include examples of verbal and emotional abuse. Provide opportunities for students to sign the display as a commitment to peaceful behaviors.

This theme could also be used in conjunction with child abuse prevention month. Provide literature or newsletter articles for parents on domestic violence, child abuse, treatment facilities, community support groups, etc

Good Deed Tree

The Giving Tree by Shel Silverstein, is one of my favorite children's stories. I have read and discussed it in a classroom guidance lesson followed by an art activity in which students cut out leaves to place on a "Good Deed Tree" in the hallway. Students are to write on their leaf a good deed they have done or plan to do. Works well in spring or fall. The leaf colors can reflect the season of the year.

Career Riddle Contest

Career awareness can be integrated into this fun learning activity for a classroom of students in grade 2 or higher. Begin by reading the class a few riddles and having them guess the career. Next, students are paired up with partners. Each pair is given a picture of a worker. They are to work privately with their partner to write a riddle about the job in the picture. Students should try to hide their pictures from others in the class. After all are finished, let pairs designate a reader to read their riddle aloud. Classmates try to guess the career.

Collect the riddles and choose some of the best to read on the morning announcements during career week/month. The first class to buzz the office with the correct answer to the riddle wins a career related children's book for their classroom. My media specialist helped supply the prize books from Book Fair overage/proceeds.

*An alternate way to begin this activity is to write the name of the career on a piece of sentence strip. Hand out names and pictures randomly and have students locate their partners by matching up. Continue with riddle writing and reading.

Below are a few sample student riddles. Theirs were better than mine.

I LOCK UP HOUSES WHEN I'M THROUGH.
I give people paperwork to do.
A SigN IN THE dirt HELPS ME do MY job WELL,
AND iF I'M LUCKY, I SELL, SELL, SELL!
WHO aM I?

(realtor)

I'M ON TV MOrNiNg aND NiGHt,
TELLiNg WHaT'S NEW aND taLKiNG jUST rigHt.
I tELL WHaT iS HappENiNg arouND THE StatE,
AND iF aN UMbrELLa you SHouLD takE.
WHO aM I?

(weather forecaster, meteorologist)

I teacH pEopLE HOW to LOSE THEir Fat.
I HELp THEM EXErCiSE UNTiL tHEY'rE FLat.
We StrEtcH our MUSCLES aND jog iN pLacE,
AND WEar StrEtcHY SUitS tHat LooK rEaLLY cutE.
WHO aM I?

(aerobics instructor)

Suggested Resources & References

Bender, J.M. (1999). *Ready... Set... Go! A Practical Resource for Elementary Counselors.* Chapin, SC: Youthlight, Inc.

Bowman, R.P & Bowman, S. (1998). *Individual Counseling Activities for Children K-6.* Chapin, SC: Youthlight, Inc.

Don't Break The Ice. Springfield, MA: Milton Bradley.

Fingerplay and Footplays. (1987). Freeport, NY: Educational Activities, Inc.

Freed, Alvyn (1991). *T.A. for Tots.* Spring Valley, CA: Jalmar Press.

Heegaard, Marge Eaton, (1995). *The Facilitator's Guide to Drawing Out Feelings.* MN: Woodland Press.

Jacobs, Ed (1992). *Creative Counseling Techniques: An Illustrated Guide.* Odessa, FL: Psychological Assessment Resources, Inc.

Lakeshore Learning Materials. Carson, CA.

Landy, L. (1984). *Child Support Through Small Group Counseling.* Charlotte, NC: KIDSRIGHTS.

La Rock's Fun and Magic Outlet. Charlotte, NC: (704) 563-9300.

Magic Coloring Book. (1977). Chicago, IL: Fun Incorporated.

Palmer, Hap. (1987). *Sally the Swinging Snake.* Freeport, NY: Educational Activities, Inc.

Piper, Watty. (1961). *The Little Engine That Could.* NY: Platt and Munk.

Seattle Public School District No. 1. (1977). *Rainbow Activities.* South El Monte, CA: Creative Teaching Press, Inc.

Senn, D.S. & Sitsch, G.M. (1996). *Coping With Conflict: An Elementary Approach.* Chapin, SC: Youthlight, Inc.

Sevaly, Karen. *Clip Art for Phonics.* Teacher's Friend Publications, Inc.

Silerstein, Shel. (1986). *The Giving Tree.* Harper Collins Children's Books.